Mighty Machines

Stock Cars

by Matt Doeden

Consulting Editor: Gail Saunders-Smith, PhD

Consultant: Betty Carlan, Research Librarian
International Motorsports Hall of Fame
Talladega, Alabama

Capstone
press

Mankato, Minnesota

Pebble Plus is published by Capstone Press,
151 Good Counsel Drive, P.O. Box 669, Mankato, Minnesota 56002.
www.capstonepress.com

1 2 3 4 5 6 11 10 09 08 07 06

Library of Congress Cataloging-in-Publication Data
Doeden, Matt.
    Stock cars / by Matt Doeden.
    p. cm.—(Pebble plus: mighty machines)
    Summary: "Simple text and photographs present stock cars, their parts, and how drivers use stock
cars"—Provided by publisher.
    Includes bibliographical references and index.
    ISBN-13: 978-0-7368-6357-5 (hardcover)
    ISBN-10: 0-7368-6357-5 (hardcover)
    1. Stock cars—Juvenile literature. I. Title. II. Series: Pebble plus. Mighty machines.
TL236.28.D64 2007
629.228—dc22   2006000505

Editorial Credits
Amber Bannerman, editor; Molly Nei, set designer; Patrick D. Dentinger, book designer;
    Jo Miller, photo researcher; Scott Thoms, photo editor

Photo Credits
Capstone Press/Karon Dubke, cover, 9, 11, 13; Corbis/New Sport/George Tiedemann, 1, 17; Corbis/New
Sport/Sherri Barber, 4–5; Corbis/Ray Grabowski/IconSMI, 14–15; Getty Images Inc./Jonathan Ferrey, 20–21;
Ron Kimball Stock/Javier Flores, 6–7; The Sharp Image/Sam Sharpe, 19

**Capstone Press thanks Gary Mueller (shown on page 13) of Chisago City, Minnesota, and Team Menard for
    their assistance with photo shoots for this book.**

The publisher does not endorse products whose logos may appear on objects in images in this book.

Note to Parents and Teachers

The Mighty Machines set supports national standards related to science, technology, and
society. This book describes and illustrates stock cars. The images support early readers in
understanding the text. The repetition of words and phrases helps early readers learn new
words. This book also introduces early readers to subject-specific vocabulary words, which
are defined in the Glossary section. Early readers may need assistance to read some words
and to use the Table of Contents, Glossary, Read More, Internet Sites, and Index sections of
the book.

Table of Contents

Speedy Stock Cars

Zoom!

A stock car races

on a track.

Stock Car Parts

The body gives
a stock car its shape.
Stock cars look a lot
like regular road cars.

Powerful engines
make stock cars go fast.
They can go twice as fast
as most normal road cars.

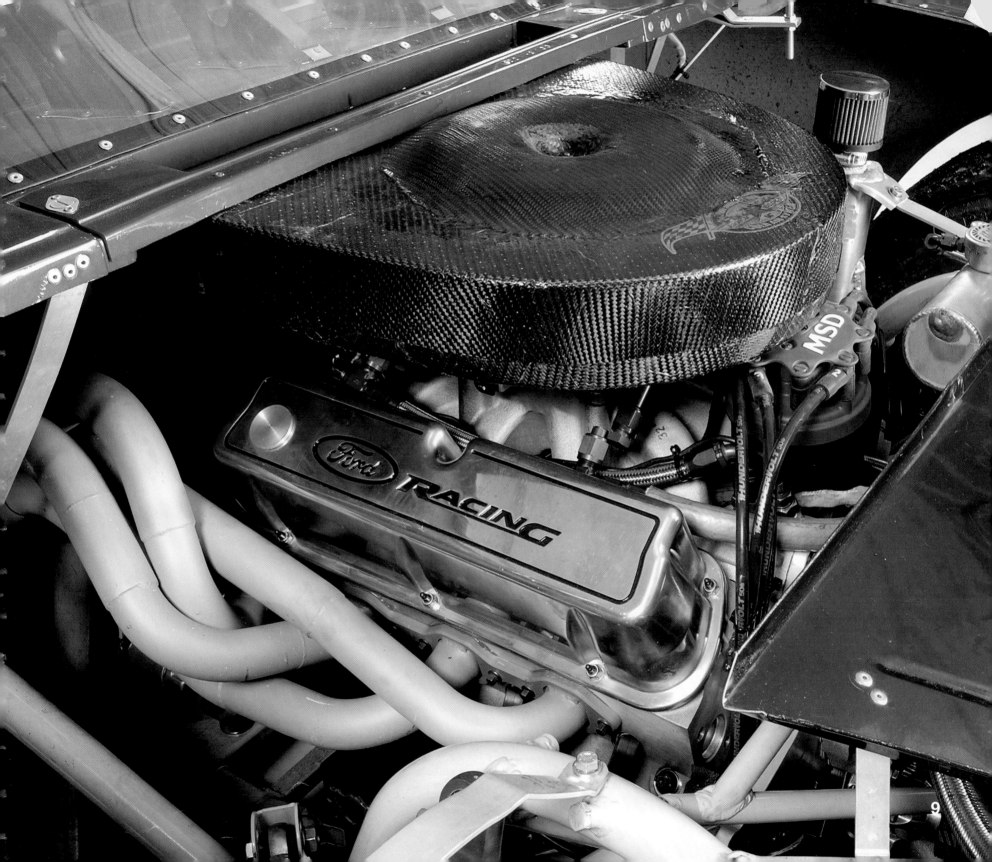

Stock car tires
are called slicks.
Slicks help stock cars
grip the racetrack.

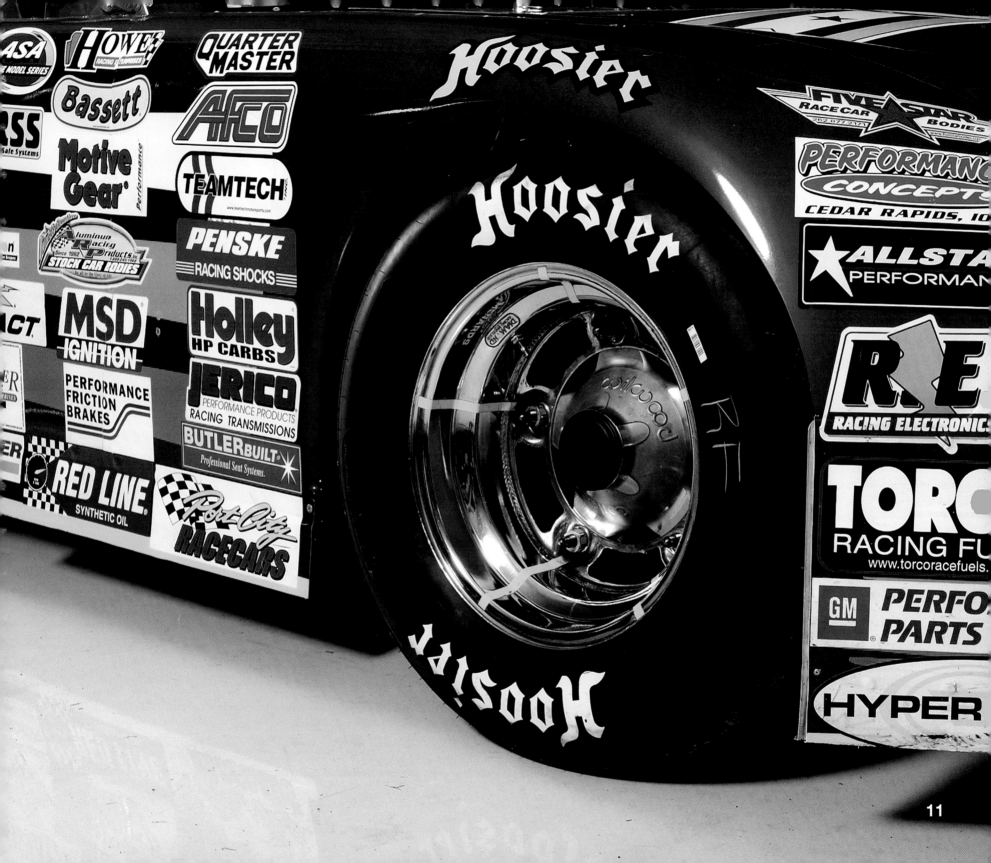

11

Seat belts and harnesses

hold the driver in place.

They keep the driver safe.

harness

On the Track

Drivers race stock cars around big oval tracks. Each race lasts hundreds of laps.

During a race,

drivers make pit stops.

Pit crews fill the cars

with gasoline.

They also change the tires.

Sometimes the drivers crash.

The cars can spin, flip,

and even catch fire.

19

Mighty Stock Cars

The fastest stock car
crosses the finish line first.
Stock cars are
mighty machines.

Glossary

body—the outside frame of a vehicle

engine—a machine that makes the power needed to move something

grip—to grab and not slide around

harness—straps that hold a driver safely inside a stock car

lap—one full trip around a track

pit stop—a break drivers take from the race so the pit crew can add fuel, change tires, and make repairs to a car

slicks—smooth tires that help stock cars grip the track

Read More

Buckley, James Jr. *Eyewitness NASCAR.* Eyewitness Books. New York: DK, 2005.

Bullard, Lisa. *Stock Cars.* Pull Ahead Books. Minneapolis: Lerner, 2004.

Doeden, Matt. *Stock Cars.* Blazers: Horsepower. Mankato, Minn.: Capstone Press, 2005.

Internet Sites

FactHound offers a safe, fun way to find Internet sites related to this book. All of the sites on FactHound have been researched by our staff.

Here's how:

1. Visit *www.facthound.com*

2. Choose your grade level.

3. Type in this book ID **0736863575** for

   age-appropriate sites. You may also browse subjects

   by clicking on letters, or by clicking on pictures and words.

4. Click on the **Fetch It** button.

FactHound will fetch the best sites for you!

Index

Word Count: 130
Grade: 1
Early-Intervention Level: 14